BOOK 7
Long -e

The Runaway Toy

ISBN: 978-1-338-57290-2

10 9 8 7 6 5 4 3 2 1   19 20 21 22 23

Printed in Malaysia   106

First printing, 2019

Book design by Marissa Asuncion

Scholastic Inc.

Andy has to **leave** for college
His toys **need** a new kid.
So **he** gives his toys
to a girl named Bonnie.

Bonnie is a **sweet** kid.
She loves her toys.

One day, Bonnie makes
a **neat** new toy.
She calls him Forky.
Bonnie loves her new toy.

But Forky does not understand
he is a toy. **He** does not know
Bonnie **needs** him.

Forky **keeps** trying to **leave**.
But Woody **keeps** bringing
him back.

One night on the way home,
Woody and Forky
go into a shop.

The shop is spooky.
Woody **needs** to **leave**.
But Forky is still inside.

The next day,
Woody **meets** Bo Peep.
Woody tells Bo Peep
he needs to find Forky.

Bo Peep knows the shop.
She can help Woody find Forky.
Together they will find
Bonnie's lost toy.

Bo Peep and Woody **sneak** into the shop.

Forky is locked in a cupboard with a toy named Gabby Gabby.

Gabby Gabby is lonely, but **she** cannot **keep** Forky. Bonnie **needs** him.

Woody and Bo Peep
free Forky.
Forky goes home to Bonnie.

But Gabby Gabby is sad.
She needs a kid, too.
Can the toys help
Gabby Gabby
find a home?

Yes, they can!
Woody and Bo find a kid
for Gabby Gabby.
It's a toy's **dream** come true!